Some Blue, a Little Spur

by Kris Falcon

UnCollected Press

Some Blue, a Little Spur
Copyright © 2023 by Kris Falcon

Cover Art: Water Dancer II © 2020, Brian Rattiner

Book Design by:

UnCollected Press
8320 Main Street, 2nd Floor
Ellicott City, MD 21043

For more books by UnCollected Press:
www.therawartreview.com

First Edition 2023
ISBN: 979-8-9883022-1-6

CONTENTS

Acknowledgments

BEFORE SOME MUD

You say there is nothing there. I see a lake,
a ferry midway toward hillocks
the boatman is sure of. Mist or no.
I see dispersing in the woods, a fistful of children
and their father or brother, seekers.
I see you heading where none disappear to,
the trails clear to all but me.
If we can dream of anything under the sun, we can
dream of God, so reads
an almanac on flowers.
It is a grower's map, rustling as I follow.
How tiresome I am, you make it known,
your back to me and some stream, smell
of sweaty mushrooms. You, carefully
sticking to "you and I" until the pickup broke down
then *you* began to sound like a curse as in
you are always eating a sandwich.
Mustard, mayo, tuna, black jack, wing, macaroni.
Less and less youthful, you.
That child you are.
Maybe I have not said a word. Letting it lag,
twisting a stem in my mouth. Dark unfolds to bare
there is nothing here. Rain gently falls its fatigue.
You might be softer now
that you are right. It is hazing up.
But doesn't that mean some mountains?
I see how I am to depart.

STREAMS ON SUBS OFF

I need the night and this city

east dissolved into air

even our darkest hour lasts 60

memory needs no originals

a "no" has no logic

you can't know the hollowness

broke as a joke but praying to be phased out by washers

that's life: to write for those who won't love you

set a sorrow free through outing a truth

an expert can mistake a song of challenge for a call of desire

for what dot over Ipsilon

that's life: mining one pain to chase away another

been a shroud a flag

comes a time to plunge into the night

ultimately alone and all else pretend

the writer could be our murderer

is the melancholia organic?

the Delta so like a plage

a song from a time I thought everyone longed to forget

am I just angry with everything, every thing that ends

he is no enigma not even a loose end

nobody does anything for nothing

one left that moves me is honesty

and the smaller this "almost" gets the clearer

let's comb whose zone

emptiness attracts wholeness

was my life was saudade

the water is yours

do we need the next fear?

what do we await to be illuminated?

there may be none riskier than a wounded boar

from the beginning a city is a street

what happens to your eye

SOME ROOM PAST 4, BEFORE 6

I crossed a square of cobras for verveine. If not a Mediterranean blue, the sky was a gray mantle on Marrakech. To drop where is beyond me, the charmers. A flicker caught my thirst.

Once, I did not make the cut to sous. I got a second call, thankfully, that I was not positive. I drank way past the sun sinking, some rounds out of despair and in between, in elation.

Circumstances had been conspiring against me, morning onward. Yet no scrap framed me in a way I could clear myself beyond doubt. I punched out early but delayed in the lobby, inhaling the smoke of accountants who offered sympathy.

Another weekend to simmer while I pureed. I played more pharmacy rock. Was fine mixing up the words as I messed up dates. Every rose has its dawn. One love, one light. No it don't Blake even.

I was in line when I was needed elsewhere. I could tell it was hard but a dog kept up with me. Told him I had nothing though like me, he would've been good with the pear in my duffel. I lost him in a square where he may have sat till late, circling his revenge.

Late lunch of dim sum, oversized view. When I flew, I took window over brut. It was this illusion I could break out, even as it made me a creature of habit. It got too late to ask for the night.

UNDER LOCKDOWN, SOME MISAPPRECIATION

We are stepping out after 36 weeks of showering
at sundown. Dear March, we are walking
past barricades right or wrong.
When we don't mean for a blur, small-winged
birds head east, cross south, dart back no design.
If a rendering, accurate. I stroke
a hollow belly. In Bangkok, it's macaques
foraging a main street in gangs. Who isn't by a sill:
nature prevails. The park seems greener
as medics pass closure,
as patrol drowns the siren with its job of denial
blaring *home* to *save lives.*
When I was nine, when power was out,
it seemed the right breadth to be told my family
tree could be traced to a foray. I've heard no clocks,
no wind vane since. My planet seemed smaller
but endless. My last chance, love reveals a new
facet every time. I turn to his profile as it dims
yet stays too warm. Deep breaths. How to suck out
the source of crimson on his pillow. Genetic,
I've read. Urban tales cry nuclear.
As if blind I feel
his right ear shaped like a sign of life.
If my heart line is pressed on his chest long enough
maybe I can catch his rhythm, a center to keep
his temple cool. I am thinking of his mother
waiting on his incisors when
his spine curves. I open our bottle
with no opener. No curveball tonight.
How down can I be for this?
We doll up like we got reservations with his chain
for time, a pocket square of lobsters to match my slip.
What is out there is the air the way
miracles take shape in water. Dear first

Friday, we leave corners lit, where fire might ward off
the brains of a troop. More sleep,
his doctor's orders. I forever clutch him close to
no atonement. Grain, grape and a river from the Alps
mix in our bodies. How to swill out, where else
can this world taste of our brines.

WEST END

Trouble is I want to be with you like this,
my arm in yours on the way to a tapas bar
as on the eve of summer
in the same breath I want to end things
(my life) not just like that
but in your arms deeper in the night, a cot death,
no sobs, your first waking thought not fault
but capacity to strive again
that mornings cradling a toddler bring.
Dig no deeper than a delusion we're free
if you ever look for my reason
for breaching. Here's my jade pendant,
a heart really a pair of carps.
I can want equally, my lone skill.
I play out the life Socrates
with you, make a lamp out of a bottle,
refresh cold opens while a ticker bends
fortunes, let lotion and balm blend, on my back
let aperitif sluice carbs,
tell myself I'm only sleeping on it but
the plan is pretty solid.
I get up at dawn to move my wet boots
from one of your corners. By the end
of December, I can only nibble sesame seeds.
There may be one step heavier before another
when furrows are uneven in the snow.
It is my mother's mother again, headed my way
whispering her daughter needs to hear this
from her child, *let them be,*
they will do as they please.

SAY NOTHING SEPTEMBER

So starved for love I don black
like a mourner. Like I'm six, unwilling to play
a candelabra. I do recite one-liners
as if on stage, that neighbor
on the phone nodding over dahlias,
yes, enough flowers, thanks.
Traitor. I am ready to dumb it down,
play it by ear, whatever won't come back
with costs I cannot trim.
Who is the smart soul, who left some vinegar
on my doorstep? Bless them early trick-
or-darers who know I'd bluff chocolate, I have
wobbled, I'm not where I say I am. With cider
I make a trap stickier than my palm for all sorts
of flies. I make a day of concoctions I won't
finish, let the ice clink May-June chimes, turn
my Long Island to a lemon.
What's the worst—there is a reason
for every fling? It is only the beginning
of a stroke of fuck? I swim many of these sunrises
where those in driving shoes would rather run.
Many ways to freshen up.
I suck it up not moaning, a dormer
again, await a shadier silence to put away
nipped stems, pistachio smells.
The season is burying me barefoot, ajar, souring
aftertastes already sore
from how it muscles what heals.

GONE, GOING

Unable to end it all we enter
Plan B, back to basics. Whiplash.
Switchblade. You make a wingspan
of two fists or are they flaring
out to firework sparks?
A vial of wolfsbane
marks my right palm red
but maybe not every bruise-blue
beauty can crack the heart.
You fled from survival from the start
where I always aimed for the jugular.
We go with whatever is darker,
every shadow a body shifting,
our solution a toxin. You've seen a lot
of drama, how common to presume
the pyro is the murderer.
A clear scent masks intent.
Suits a funeral as much as a wedding
like a dahlia. You take off our gloves.
Try not to perspire. I am
down to our last fume.

OVERWATER OUTLYING

The pair of horses you carved from your shell
Your ballads on a cove you swore you found in me

Fuck your sorry you never mean

You can drift with your paddles and nets I'm good
with a ball bouncing back rounds of pelota
the click after parentheses Rock salt off
all pretzels off all crackers

In every palm a red weevil Stillborn berry
Lead gushing into gangrene   The mirror
wrinkling stares to white strands Many endings
are omens by your side

Is the desired a reward if it inflicts pain

Fuck your fake "lost" without you Fuck your roasts
Fuck all your *Promise* Your last crust you fed me as it got dark
You scraping off your tattoos because they were not my initial

First I screamed until dear echo
broke the universe I supposed
settling a score for me Cloud-shaped rustling
shaded tears Sun dusted my footfall gold

There is no timetable for tides You can turn
your minute back You can choke on your bamboo bong

Some days obscura Many years a journal has more focus
Nights I walk until convinced I am reaching an edge
of the world where the island began I thought
when you held me

When you find me here you can keep
your one-way ticket

Fuck your space you keep showing off
The sun dial you dug on my hill
till your fingers bled the right hand

11

AFTER YOU LOST YOUR WAY

Storms ravaged your village on Twin
Lakes, landing a day apart as only they could.
I had just pushed you back to your mother's
milk button, wide sleeve, sure hideout.

I was stirring a clove of garlic in tomatoes
to counter fever, bloat your belly
when I didn't ask why you were hiding in Chicago.
Before we badmouthed loves then did not. Bits neither
dark nor light. I could've called. I had forgotten the name
of an endangered mammal in your mountains,
same hills you smoked until everyone smoked there then
stopped. Some are saying you're no free spirit, you

just fell for a child. Power cut for a year on your rock
and my love adds, zip chance of getting solar.
Without a place, it may be lighter to go vegetarian,
unmask. It's hard to watch a graying cat

without relating a panther
that prowls my dreams. It may be you who said I was
my own distraction or did you mean
deconstruction. Pauses were views
from a balcony, easy. I often believed you had it wide.
Aren't you the lastborn, your own ocean,
chronicler, were you not to be wisest? Still trying to stir
in sleep with my prong. It sure feels like day seven.

MISSING THE SOOT IN THE SPUR

There may not be music in your heart
though a song from childhood drifts
ahead of grief so you cannot ever be
wholly in the dark, come crack- melt- downs.
Sometimes you catch the doors with your fray
of a fate line, out of breath at the buzzer.
Sometimes you keep your head down, conscious
of your pace in deja vu, now
only good as never when you pull out
like an expert hand on diffusing.
Either way, you figure it out after
what has been foreseen fulfills
yet the heave of rush hour screens
that starless ceiling you don't have keys to.
Aperture night. Not to correct
is to let it unfold. Amateur rings.
You have always just beached but your face returns
ashen, you cannot scatter enough. Do you feel
like filing a leave again with a sure end,
beginning? Maybe a gap semester come break,
solo bites, a chance to step into those striped
boots you coated carmine, find a crystal
bell inside the smallest nesting doll.
Flawless slice, thinnest line. At last
to go unsigned on abecedarians.
You want to keep it silent in your rental
all the way to a memorial's gate. Enough
where you are versus what tingles.
Your fingers check the dashboard
for dust, as if to smooth the sun. You think
you care. Yet you won't angle
a mirror to your vision.

DAY OF ANTITHESIS

My host's log seems for two: fish eels by brunch.
Lunch onward, devise wails to drive out weevil
orgies rotting palms.

Sounds like a mother whale, but I am too near.
My silence feels ever smaller. My days till zero
spent slanting where I can't translate—

> moon or demons
> I take clarity by the capsule
>
> who doesn't fall for a prophet's voice
> in the interior
>
> calls warm from palo santo
> of hunger fogging up
>
> into a fugue bearing one
> tearing others who rely on ardent thighs

ASKED FOR SEA VIEWS, I HEAD FOR ABSTRACT

First stop, my first school of dove-white blooms, midday
sun melting a capital elsewhere. My tallest wish
sang to my lightest shadow. Blessings meant a lake—
not parts but whole. Every boat of mango free of carbides.
My rice I greased with golden juice
I later learned was water. Much later: "she is wondering
whether to join." A crosswalk glistened at the end

of long blocks. Yet what lasted were songs belting
love of what leaves the earth. I killed time knowing
the words while Thea watched capers. I followed
like a little sister, tanked a plastic tea cup.
A fighter from a forgotten war is cast inside a wall
as if to be jettisoned. Like blackmail
nudes lodged in a brain. Every dream means none of this

fabric makes a hue. No lifter, criers by a bay.
Just a pew with a patient, once an underling still
asking a coroner, *how do you not tremble?* Who takes
to a dome now, fresco of wings faded from pleas.
I am being trusted here for my capacity to be
certain the robin has the boldest heart. A map
on my palm stings right. Every branch toward the waves.

IMPORTANCE OF HUNDRED PERCENT

When I quit quitting is when I opt out. The catch
to wider space, I can taste it all. I cannot narrow
to one way, the landscape to fit. There is blood where bread is.
A surrogate who crashed my cabana is still falling off a cliff. A
closer barely eats, agonizing over a pet he left in the middle
of the Atlantic. Has it found a shore? A pensioner
pays to quote on happiness for hours. But it is *Blaise*
I can't turn over or around. I whisper

the tag in my head until russet oozes.
It is not hard to write off pursuing what you want
when you shift and sleep in the same station,
avoid pains of flight. My flash off, I have been playing tourist
with some conscience. I purchased a Chagra to set it free
or let it be devoured in the wild. Everywhere, triangles.
What is so crucial about saving a spirit, even if this may be
a devil's? I stroked his chin before he or I faded. He may have tried

to look me in the eye. In dreams I am in a lab coat
on the stones a village was slaughtered. Questioned,
I dare not falter on the anthem. A blade inside my mime's cane
drops and I seize from my diaphragm. I studied on this square.
How to be limber enough to dodge. Happiness
is not in the present. Blaise in the halls, whistling. My breath
holds looking for a mirror, each relief intricately carved
from gold and blood, none mine, to be certain.

HIATUS

I debated for so long I stepped out with no view
past pall shrouding the skyline up to airspace
to Dippers I may have dreamt when I was small.
I am never finding answers
to give a child. I drove to cane fields I mistook for corn
before I could be seen stuttering in the city.
How quickly fall out spirals to fall from grace.
I was watching the world rend, where I could have been
broken and still caught demons unmasking a godfather.
I thought I was gifted a secret ingredient.
A sliver of astrophyllite in my left palm
came free with amethysts.
I was to reflect on ruin I brought, down to transmissions
slippery under my reign. I was to sprawl on the lawn, listen
silent as a sallow key past tuning.
Some are born yang to oro, plata. I respect
the gleaning life like a night of love.
Sync to the few who follow
three steps to feel whole. No chain of command.
Begin with an herb with prayers might flower,
the scrying freebie on my right ear.
Borrowed hose, brook water, seed bed.
Sometimes I rip thorns, strip weeds,
I was to wash up scuffed.

FOSTER-EYED

You will never know where it comes from,
how you want to vanish but need to be moved.
How a life of speaking low sets you at high altitudes
you are excused from demands of time—
Right. Faster. Left. Slower.
Master of effect if not cause (gravity), you know
which pawn keeps an icepick on the way up.
Secrets are a hazard to precision
but the lone lullaby you give away
is a fresco of cotton clouds
when the headmaster pulled a switch, willing you
asleep sooner, let them see you were taught as a child
to genuflect. Yourself a solace
you appear to float behind your sunglasses
before you sharpen to focus,
your grip solid as you map out
the next step while the players lounge, listening to
their dreams or following the heart, a privilege
of descendants who change their minds.
That time you were told to remember, let
the milk flow until it doesn't.
You sign away your initials, those of an heir
to no one, hole-schooled. Connect bullet
points you just do not do, unable as you are to send
regrets or thanks. Yet you are heard knowing all
the words you sing, as if your head depended on it
or to keep yourself from hurling,
brightly. To the sky, a ceiling you blow.

COMEBACK LIKE LAST WORD

Coming back means having to come through,
scan with winnowing eyes.
Rise with early runners as if good
intentions disperse the cloud in your lungs.
No turning as you are commended,
the polyglot who grows ecotherapy.
Instead, a step forward when asked on your 25%
to make relay, same tone for so are you trying
for a baby. Your eyes have gone underwater all year,
they could stare down a hound to let
your headlights through. You can let well
-wishers peer at your just-sprinkled beds,
let the disarmed toast your cooling, sparkling drink.
Remember the kid from a lower grade
who liked to invent he was there, who forged
assorted names for an imaginary friend?
Except you really have been, have you
to Kerkennah, Tyrrhanea.
How long through that sea, submerged
before you surfaced? You dried your soles
on the shore's hot nuggets. How many times
saved while you spent each return
like water. Before spiritual, science you
ritualized. Lung before whole body.
Maya blue your gaze drank, those skies
gauged salt in the sapphire depths, on your tongue.
Where there were cliffs, you dove.
You would not listen for the cords to click
but there was no godmother to switch
valves with. *Vamos a ver.* No flinching
as a capsule you took with no spritz floats
in your gulf. Whatever sprouts you bet your body
can best. Again, you dive.

LAKESIDE

Your profile less silhouetted here, fishing four hours
        away from the city bay, down a lagoon
reflecting shifts, as I cushion a bombshell
        with defensible faults you have on me. That year
I let drift a driftwood raft, answering to no
        one, sliding from screes I drank on. Another
eighteen months I went by a voice
        lifted from a pirouette.
Wads, sachets in the pocket of ferns, sage.
        I fall for an impulse to turn moments to a totem
every time, I crave like a mother-to-be craving
        grapefruit first, leopard prints next.
Tell me if you can bear it, bear it. An ordeal
        can be endured where there are ferry hours.
My top and skirt are not from the same black
        ensemble. They belong in the hamper of a widow
deep in debt. Except I rest first—
        How to sleep longer than you. I could blink
my eyes to shut but my body would still shiver
        from the cold of our lake. Of storms, I cling
to odds. Each oar, I forge back its oldest crest.
        Some phoenix I would make.
You measure margin, the pinnacle
        from feet. Core from teeth. Your timing from
the clef seamless as I run out of time.
        You are called by your birth, your one name
my prayer to start over, old way to cry out, like a little girl
        out of wolf. Because I haven't a clue how
you will be. A yellow leaf falls to the water,
        a lily for a second.
You are more placid than your shadow, the only
        abstraction you give away.

BEFORE YOU MARK AS SAFE

You are like those principals serenaded with single-origins
who turn a house into a mausoleum of their forefathers'
angers, frosting into bitter pits, sporing
as much hate as can be inhaled. Your two
journals blur like -ember months. Once for eyeteeth
nightmares, one to scrap inventions for the iris.
Fires feeding fire. No warmth comes from ether.
What mad groove do you sleep in where you meet
every query on whereabouts
with a timetable for tides, the horizon line?
Maybe you like swimming in your fleece
because you can still hear your last hound bark.
You think you mean it, but if odds were in your favor
you would have a home with a dock. Sculls
lean behind the kitchen door where a broom should.
You search for an herbarium to douse what grows
green again in the fumatorium.
Heliotrope sprouts through a raft
you left in a field of cobalt and cinnabar flora.
How violet light has grown on you as you dig
small graves in a lost cave.

LATE INTAKE

The last time I was as thirsty I had claimed a lie,
a big lie I wept about for days softly, an intern again, micro-dosing
after being found out, before being shunned.
I don't know what self-harm or whatever stopped. But I clambered
on a beach hoppers' bike with damp hair.
I still ask for tiger prawn, a special there, whenever
lobster is offered. I still look for the Maria
in my name. All my names mean alegria, aching for a smile.
Macrame lace I slept in left filigree on my back.
Bines warping a forsaken wing.
A whipped oak I wanted branded on my cheek. I was nowhere
to be found when families, orphans, gazed into a just-set sun
like they could the bottom of a quandary. I scanned
faces until a language sounded like my sister's voice.
The more steps, the more cracked shells
scratched like nails. Too late to take cover
when the weather turned and vomited rain after rain. The Pacific
could not hold in any differently, wave after wave.
I meant to bring home a surf. I serve everything like ice cream,
upside down. A paddle rests on a couch I sleepwalk to.
My left calf
knows a rolling pin. I would call my child after a city
I have been presumed from. Half checked out, there is no moral
behind the murals. As it is, osmosis, saline.
There is no tool to prepare for certain questions. Where my blood
flows from, for whom I grew up, where the ones
I loved most survive.
Trust me only when every inch is cold, I am writing
on May from February.

SLUICES MORE GRAY THAN RED

Nodding slowly like I'm getting a mime, about to give
change for a vibe more than the act
though I haven't reached for my pocket,
the eternal teen I have been, tossed keys
to an endless midsummer, noblesse
oblige worn well, spiked seltzer downed
to find if it warms or cools the body, which bay
I am unable to sense.
Nothing to blurting out one name instead of another.
Nothing to skimming to the end to see
an arc through, getting to the heart of an apple
with a cleaver. Even I believe I am conceding
when I consent,
later convenient over *never*. As a child I was
taken to ice I mistook for marble countertops
I mistake for a seabed.
Reward was descent. The whoosh down was called
devil's noise but the bowels of earth were
far from hellfire, closer to meltwater.
Into rivulets, I dropped a wish.
I know my limit
spelled out in waves on my electrocardiogram.
When a lane cracks to no
portal, riders have an ocean in mind.
At plume, it's a crimson feather in mine.
I can be any port I want, I was told on a rooftop
left with a windup face to feel a ploy
out of time. I'm skipping to the murmur I fade.

DAY OF THE EASED OUT

Algorithms sift lapses now, even this
hand out a window trembling.
These hands, there is ever less need for the spine
and spread. Logging hazards again, flights to
landscapes I am never landing. How to switch off.
New rhythms pedal the cycle. This cycle, a blur.
I take to a fragment up there—
a hawk no one hunts, unwitting master
of the drain atop manors.
From the ground, its span is the sky
when done with its job. Nowhere between exact
and asylum. There is ever less space for a nest
as time runs out. No matter how early I jog,
an elderly chastises
the graveyard is not a park. I have yet to sync
with a friend's period.
I skip my horoscope for my last love's
that happens to be the weather I wish
to heed, a brilliant sail.
A load off not to be queried are you able
to fly soon, yet even the back of my mind
bends from the pressure of absence. Mindset,
often the last to know. Out there: fast.
Indoors: this face. Who counts peak moments
of imprudence? Where a brace should be,
a lamp turned back to a crystal of rum.
Where dishes should not mold,
my good white shirt. I watch
a blue stain ruin the linen uniform.
It is an old whodunit in my petite castle
between liquid and detergent, I'm leaning
toward water, a bit of river ink.

WHICH ERA DID YOU WANT TO LIVE IN?

It is not your pace I fail
to keep up with. I understand I mistake
moves from A to B for steps 1 and 2.
I drive until I break down.
When to warn you I won't be here for apocalyptic
rain. Do you feel me here?
Strip tease till my top is off. The drink minimum
my max. Burlesque in a ruin.
Before you I crashed in a basilica wishing
I had not so quickly gathered my belongings, fled,
and dwelled in my chair instead
as a starfield burned. Until a fire
in the forest swallowed my smokes.
Where are those souls who double back
to stop someone from passing?
Not every traveler plots to conquer
in peace. Let me walk by you
in a field again, nothing less than your ally
nudging you to inch closer,
neither an expert on escape, just a couple
on the way to a planetarium to make out.
Let us through, we won't blink
on a radar. We're just a pair of this world spinning
bulletless and the roulette.
Undressed for the northern lights.

FIVE IN TRANQUILITY

I did open. I daydreamed. My fingers moved over the motif to see
 the hand that painted.

Entry was free. Spent on: a pass, crossing a border overnight.

I was the one who called I was also the vandal

I dressed up for the oath part.

Screaming at the resort's security startled a senior to hiccup to his
 grave

Maestro, I really did not know where my tab went.

I wanted to marry in the capital to feel defined in the infinite
 underneath the copula

The half was less when I returned

I go back to the last page of his last book where it states where he
 lives since I stated in writing he did not leave voicemail.

Because I was still home. Because I think of vitamins at *spectrum*

Because it was an era I went by an alibi

Yes I was not as tired as I could have been bolder

Fear for my life made me disrobe and hand my satchel over

Milk tasted like someone had been living out of the carton.

I had no designs on a spire spun from lies

I KEEP MYSELF ALONE FOR YOU

Bathing with my bowl. Hedging paths
from the water. The engine plucked out.
Not your picture of lonely as you
left, sulking by a dock.
I am not yet hooked to the point of empty.
There is time to plan a picnic. Let me
glimpse the age you believe
your voice belongs to. Amber light on
champagne sheets. Lush lair to unfold in, save
the wrinkle of your shape. Finding
the fjord to your pace, I paint this egress gray.
Scent that porch Aubade. A butterfly
sips from a thistle. I pick a tide with a good chance
of storm to latch you in. Then a moonless walk.
I paint over often.
Not every fantasy about the future
tempts into deceit.
To receive I hold it in longer,
cross-legged like a woman with a pink line
on campus, listening to swan songs.
How many dreams of you
come unclouded with your face I'm forgetting,
your breath real as an orphan's, poised
to dive or take flight.
I sleep with my lipstick on again. *Red halo.*
Switch scarves with my lamp.
I pray the universe would beckon to you then
but you are kept on your way loosely
buttoned, flown to yesterday. You unfasten to be
flung like a disk back into the night.

MISSING A CONSTELLATION

I may have been happy watching the river ice.
Where are those voices who love
to stir, "speak your truth!"

My turn at the counter.
I give the name of a stillborn I kept.

Sometimes it helps to put up a love's photos
as if to solve a mystery. At 20

I had a little spur. I felt more compassion
than anybody for a man who hired three
strangers. To endure a good beating. To see

if he'd talk. I make fourth in my corner.
What is weariness from cycles called?

I am *blank*, I claim in a circle around
an imaginary pyre, trying to hide my breath

from the cold with a bubble jacket.
I flash my pass for a skyway like
it is a passport to cross over.

CHIMERA

When you were orphaned you fled
the hills. You climbed up to a terrace
to tiptoe down a pantry, squeeze into
a shelf for half-moons. You had not been told
the rain, oceans, are not fountains.
Your detector found a coin on the compound.
You started to believe a little, even
remember, even as the bed padding the sea
kept sinking, where you belonged. Cliffsides were
hunts you harnessed. No grotto was spared.
You would be no different. You would dream, too
to be encircled. For a loaf, you borrowed customs,
the closest to virtue you'll know, prayer
a stone on the tomb of those who sold you
bulbs that died tulips, served their fresh brews,
who feared you were still *there* when
you could not be *here*. For whom yin & yang
ping-pong till blip more gray than red—
is there another world?
Someone who swallowed what could not be
snuffed out to blend in. The few who desire
not as metaphor long
to see their fires feed in you no other
fury but light, long to relive an interment for
the beloved, a day in mute violence.
Crackers remain runes. A fading
cypher you took as warmth because you were
the size of a palimpsest. How your voice lost
the pearl in your anthem, but how well one hand
baited as the other knotted,
no lens fogging over your eyes.

"TURN TO NATURE"

Do we not mean waves coming for footsteps too,
the stone in our stream, scarring walls?
If every surface meant exit, ineffable

light. If any silence could be a mirror. Lone
window latched all summer. The glare
on beeches by Calame.

A moored gaze.
A languid lake, once a dam
where we can count on catch to taste like a ripple.

If it be simpler to have a whisperer set us
in a whirl. We start old until we are done.
First, fin. Then find how *fin* rings true, too.

Banaba, some midnights. At the root of intake,
a sprout. Late lunch, verbena. Many names
for an infant should a spirit come.

Do we mean to keep an eye out
for a fading sun's orb, a brief horizon
on our horizon?

ASKED TO DRAW MY FACE

Windows like this I've proofed good
all my life. Irreversible, confirms science,
same brackish foam where the hemisphere may be.
None of the elms can be heard
before a downpour. I regret a little.
They line my lane up to the main road. I would trade
the moon ever missing to hear again, not to draw from
the top. Wherever I land I face north. Common mistake—

silent: still. I don't listen for a leak in the wall
but wheeze. I am just about done holding my breath
for a beat. To even. Who can't tell burn from reflux but
thoughts of a puddle on fire put off sleep. Disquiet
yawps on, itches, impossible to locate.
What a pain (I am) to clutch on when nothing goes down,
something on my left half gives, a pinch at a time.
Intermittent flights of small birds

can lift like dragonflies in May, the spirit. A bit.
Retreat from haze, they could. Found a pair once,
thought I could bring one back.
Who has the strength to return to its body, who hums
to hear the other lilt as it slips?
Maybe hurt only harms.
My canal fills toward dusk with ducks
pairing off to a dark soiree.

EVERY STONE IS FOR GROUNDING

Would that be fuel, filling across the river
a red tower? My wish was

        to live on water
I would not come back from, pupil or prophet.

I turned from a road that seemed endless
        it could only parallel the way I was seeking.

Re-peeled. Sarong on a ghost chair
faced upstream. But I put off swim class. My back

to attacks *too much a romantic* or *why won't*
        you save a cynic? Compete? Waking mid-shower

        maybe I doubled in a last life. Well-heeled
in a high-rise, I veered off

        where a coast shimmered as a beach. You'd have
cheered. Where banks accreted a sidewalk a day

        from overflow. Levels I need not heed.
        Where long naps ended like laps with a love

        I am not vacant, calling me to shore.
As it is, barefoot, must halve empty. My skirt blown

        nowhere, anyone's road wrap above.
Re-vaulted. Much of here depends on the nerve

to show up. The feet to sweep away sugar, salt. A dredge
sifts what a throat could have swallowed.

September, the door lets in a puddle, lost,
clear path before a dam siren reaches.

LIGHTER REDS, FADING BLUE

I've switched my route to graffiti where
storefronts would drop
spiked blends to laced Wellies. What you take?
warped to where you at? real quick. How often
have I gauged force wrong. One in five stops
at a child blindfolded with a mirror
not to be seen, the way zero say something
with the same zipped stillness I hoped it was nothing—
a foreman a few weeks back
tossing bones like beams in a pile.
I was carrying bougainvillea like they were
lilacs in a vase, to the crypt.
My great-greats understand
I grow no shade, rain or shine. And take
no cover. The stenciled waif sheds chalk.
This hot, how do kids still shoot out on a lawn
even if it's paint
or water. It would take more than
an art to get me cracking. To *forge from verge*—
from one kid. I was more a pills person, out like
a light three days,
how an embryo might slumber on
to fetus or succumb.
Who wants to know? soon to get lost in
who isn't the city? Here is that ash on my fingertip.
Chrysanthemum in hand. My head still damp
in a towel, same threadbare rag
for a small fire.

OUTSKIRTS

The wind, a field soughing calls to return.
Rain, the night rinsing the earth's
ribs to atom.
What further message to be divined?
        I reject a search party. Once,
I lived to swerve.
Radio remains on my handlebars.
But I still sleep all day to get up for head count,
eyes rested for a hunt.
Skin taut as a portal to be entered.
Wherever I have driven to, I am asked
        are you able to bend?
I punch more holes for beans. Yes
        I am blacking out till I am gone.
I feel for debris from kayaks, a campfire,
a purple sky that did storm, drusy
on cinders, paraffin, rosin,
feathers with the blood
from belly and paw, callings of survival
        too late to land.

THE HEART HAS NO PLACE

The plague minds no time
as if ablaze. Who has no pulse, burn.
Where four may mourn, burn a vigil around
an orchid. Vespers cannot be heard
without a body, even with each corner filled.
Delinquent: a breath.
Who step out for ball mime penalty
shots at yard time, the tension all in a cleat,
any pretend shot, doomed.
Who dare a kiss are fined, queue outside
the town hall to bake at noon. Heat—
accessory to the noose, survivor
of pyres. Summons muffle
the rattling doors to court.
No knot to be done or undone. Small squinting
smaller. Chamber by chamber switch a lamp off
as if for Earth Hour, belated shows
of solidarity. Better waitlisted than
never—hotel beds turned back to a hospice.
A church back to a crypt. Departure
less lonely. When nothing needs hinging,
crib to chest, a joiner and his son wait
for the minibus or an angel to speed up an end
either way to hunger. Last two in this world
who remember how
wake once meant a watch.

A WHOLE OUT FOR AN ANSWER

When you say you are certain, everyone
in the room looks that direction for the wind
to prove most insatiable.
A garden you broke into growing up
grew only annuals.

The clouds do not gather over you.
Must be how you receive messages
so clearly and still. You are yourself
like a gleaming zone just mined, can't be dulled in
a drawer with a key. Light to end half-life for.

Do you ever linger for an edge you can break?
Of all selves, you let in your 12-year-old, raven-
clawed in the left half, still intact
yet ahead of the curve inside
your crow center, pricking, bleeding.

OUTSIDE THE HEXAGON

called to the paddocks you are found at sea
again aiming for shearwaters
who spreads the wax on their feathers hears them
augur rain
whether for birdsong or the mounts you leave to their circles
you sprinkle grain like you would cast alms in a well
for an echo

heart and head align on a summit with the itinerant
with the poet hunger wolfs down headlines on hunger
to sleep under a star

whoever spars in your head pedals to condemned grounds
where even the fire escape was left behind
the fallowed you find
nothing looted from this kingdom you crank it up
until you step on every shard you would not know
none is a relic

by the third warning you're a champion
at games of outrunning
sometimes you are saved by a mesh
sometimes silence is
revving room for the abrasive it feels almost
like a weight to smother you
in your sleep to keep you from dreaming
in looms

you still wish to see the shape your life takes to fly you out
who hopes the gut has the balls
to pull a trigger

no AWOL is worse than one of a student who takes
with the break ending with the town to be razed

38

the first train back to the city
you suck on a splinter from a placard
close to your collar hold your breath
you are still in a cloud of attar

HERE NOWHERE

That time I got lost too easily, so often I relied
         on directions, my memory good when spoken to.
             Forked roads untangled with a widow's rant
         on needles. Sang to me as I followed a trail
         of fallen fruit, how before a railway freedom
protests braided into love songs. The nurses left.
                 Metro art lines a terminal now, a tunnel,
         any bridge vandals named theirs. Here, fun—
in a dilating iris, waves. A bejeweled brain. Steep roofs
         are small flights. A wall of moringa, some proof
             villages outnumber the city. I am counting riders
         on their way to work, racing past a skull
in a straw hat mistaken for a scarecrow or
             offering. I nod back *never* [forget] *better.* Deep
divers keep out this far. Though a swamp to the undertow
tests positive for massacres, next year's inevitable
             drought. I pray to the guardian angel for
             repenting in the valley, the same charm
for bargaining, for keys with which I can crack
         a cocoon for the night.
                 Effigies seep through a lease assured
bullet- flood- proof on deposit. I have not run. Redeem
         I don't. Mothers maybe, railing against an example
         made of a rager. How signals were clear
            when there were still great-grandmothers.
         When a stray howled, the third would be for a woman.
Neighbors who hear over the highway keep
their dog in. There, done.
         Foragers sleep through banging pipes, clattering canes,
            undersides where I lose count.

MOVING ON

Staying in. A new sink. Letting leftover
smells lint to grime. The body's warm hollows.
Who can say who unscrewed the blinds
but I keep all that can be crawled through shut.
Until most day is down and a mailbox,
driveway, the nearest elm mark a road, that much
accord. Until a rush of wind let in is like
a gasp, like enough, if this is all I will know.
It is just before dark when I shed my clothes.
Do some washing while bathing, a faint
conscience reminds. The shutters frame
me, lab mouse in a bungalow,
yet those vague shadows in the loop do not
slam me obscene. With their hunched
shoulders, what could they want they would
not guess, mint skates in my closet?
I sewed long ago my diamond
in the belly of milkfish.
It's harder to keep it simple or *I dare you to
show how much more you ache* they try
to read me right, whispering all the way
home to sour soups, not more enlightened.
Tomorrow another sight unseen.
Tomorrow my cousin who stirs stock,
vaccinates pets, just won't phone.
I will give it courtesy minutes by the curb
with a bucket. Any piece of fabric can look like
a body after a storm. A leather slip-on
drunken off a motorbike.
An undershirt whipped from a ledge.
Garden gloves slit rinsing
a child's fork. I don't believe in warming
paunches. I pour in my oldest crystal my last kick.

Pull one more sound, no stranger
to me, a curtain through a rod.

MISSING SOME BLUE IN THE GREEN

The city has no yard. A boy learns to play
a song with glasses of water, a spoon.
To sound like a xylophone if he can't like the ocean.
When nothing trickles from a drum
or the sky, he drinks his wells. Before any turns
vapor or wine he empties until
he hears his voice. Tiny pool, drop of a cent.
Maybe it's as close as he can be. Here's to prayers
for elsewhere, to be someone else, even
from a carrier of the new lethal running
for shade, crushing mimosa.
Slowing the world down.
Clouds will not shift back to shape.
Who has faced the ask for otherwise
cannot help but bargain. Runners up
who do not see through the end watch,
mute behind tinted forts. Every night is
an all-nighter, burning where it does not add up.
Lenders who count on no visit
flower a path though they can cut to any corner,
no snag. A lot of using goes on as much as good.
Dreamers who sleep all day
sleep through the first audit. A blistered palm
finds moss along the ramparts. To cushion
a fall? How many shortcomings in a setback?
But it is getting easier embracing
abstract, the town pantry full,
loving like an aunt or brother. Then like a son,
a rival, the other end of a transceiver, so on,
a bully with his arm left to twist.

AUGUST INTO WHATEVER IT WAS

It pulled as if I could lend a hand
mooring me so there was no room to muse,
will this come my way again?
I eyed my pace as if I were behind a step
already headed to a trance where I could
vanish. A lover was involved. A reversible jacket
in a city ditched by labor, a cafe thinned to vape.
It landed a beauty first, light
as barbs on a blond shaft, so swiftly
my heart leapt to a gap once molar.
His faults startled in small currents, no way not to be
swept along before a mother flaw burst, roles
blurred, wound me down until I let drift,
done with play in a loaned home, dried
and sewn again for love to find
some tides later, cooler nape in a walk with him
all it was, butterflies flown, why italicize what
is known, his voice aligned with his gaze his torso
assured of being desired back the rest of
the breathy breeze I floated on day
long undulating veil slowing with me
why not once more or longer or sure flip
sounds of a flounder in a bucket one side gleam
one side starless *too soon too soon*
tang back in tangent the distance cooling shimmers
to blind or be saved
hieroglyphs at once tongues
mere ripples onward away—

WHEN THERE'S NO CALLING BACK

Find confession where
porcelain crashes. Furies bottled
        as fear. Whisper in your shed
the measured way you coax a cry
        to leak out. Clear a bench,
let winds rock a swing, wherever
        you would linger if you wandered.
But grab your seat from your nook.
        Wait for sconces in the house
to come on as you do the dark at sundown.
        Drink up like you are grateful
toasting an empty pool
        like you spend afternoons filing
a tool in the garden.

NEW YEAR'S NOTE

What follows "Listen"
can wait. I have not drawn open the curtains as wide
since a Doberman fought with a Shepherd.
       Tonight, the woman with the louder bark is burying
       sharp edges. Her loose end? Did she wish for radio

silence, smooth around the curves left? No new moon to spot
her fossils. But her pistol tops the mound as a firework jolts
       midnight with comets. Launch costs

as do defenses. Does she feel savage with no tweezers?
       Listen, I'm just living my platform. What to do
          but keep my shadow out of sight.
I have lit the patron saints. I will see myself off
to catch a one-act from my box.

       Some trees of the fig family are for the spirit
          to unfurl, some for winds to blow about, howl on,
            let stalks overrun the bough. *Listen.*

Unarmed, the woman is a no-show
for the salon or contracts. She walks her champion
early. Sick leave rounding off to gap year.
       She circles our roundabout like it's too small
          to drown in, but large enough for a race.

FOR A FRIEND OFF COAST

The captor's head throbs, speaking of wildebeests
and crocodiles coming up on wildebeests at the lake
every June. The captive sobs
how long do I have here?

The odd, flickering phantoms they make. Two wrecks
cracking up or in a quarrel like children fresh out
of camp, finding the field again to the road.

They take turns acting warden. Squinting strains
the eyes until the throat is parched.
The need to be sharp by nightfall
when directions arrive suspends trouble

mounting from a language barrier.
One offers a bottle, the other pours the water
away as if it were poison to spit out.

They wait for the eve so long it gets hazy who
cuffed a compass. Why they steer away from the sun.
Whose lover ratted and whose masterminded.
They are at it again with the rods. The chase always

the cut. One mate picks up steel like a wand
and the second mate, like a fossil,
hungers taking over an instinct to flee.

IN THE DARK, THERE IS NO HALF

Part of it earthlight keeping the moon's face in the shade.
Sometimes it's hard to close a loop. If you can't say anything nice…
Do unto others… Where is the chorus to aver in unison?

A performer friend starts each riddle yelling on a sidewalk.
Even among hatchet guys, surely somebody wants to free a firefly
for 50 cents. Her box still smells of cigar from a slots job. Her trick
so light nobody hears if the cage is hollow. She is no longer told

less little girl, please. I have no other life but I understand
those ones flying high on a double life. My key is also my saw.
Dreams of chase, I barely budge till there is no way but to fall.
My seer friend—sun-streaked noon to my bleary-eyed eves. She
cannot sugarcoat how the cycle where only I see

a design will only have answers for everybody but me.
I inch closer, as if promised a sphere in a theater to swallow me
and every outsider and their doubles and halves whole. Destined
to play out centers, my friend. She can take off plastic from all

seats in one tug. When it rains, her glove keeps her pet dry.
Apologues cannot be rushed. She says it is possible some are a side
in a puzzle but most are made of many loose ends.

WHITE SCREEN

I can go three movies more a day from salty, tart
to saccharine, slacking till my head draws a blank.
Till jingles for children soothe into
a *land of curves and curls*, an instinct to start over
black & white. An artist's in a mother's life:
mask chemicals with onion soup.
She dims her kitchen back to a dark room.
Her son who suffered
an explosion takes shape in a pan.
A deserter saves a widow's daughter
on the other side with all he knows
of their anthem. His neighbor snipes his nape
in error. For rabbit stew, chef plays hunter
coaxing ferrets to the ground.
I want to agree with After on a yard
makeover, the clean slate a hedged verandah,
the fresh door bluebird-blue if refuge
is real. My halluces fit at the drought's most humid.
If I keep flipping, my signal should pick up snow—
not a bleached stage
for a bloodbath, no metaphor on a bleak future
but August 5th on Esquiline hill, mist me
a miracle mousse, cushion for all,
an immaculate carpet made of flurries, for ash,
show me the slush that keeps slipping back
as flakes descending on a silent night, score
settled like a phantom
horseman with his head back on, enough
for the ill to stay in, disremember, to be beyond
again, my smallest, gills in a silver lake.

PRESSED FLOWERS

I pocketed love letters when
I was slipped mine. Volumes not composed
in return. I watch how animals feed,
flee, which shrubs blossom, are consumed,
are regrown. Where? How? When? Bloom.
Love, I have professed only mid-argument—
We'll never be even. We won't
feel the same at the same time. Like a
chapter on piquancy
in a history of oils. The longhand
spanning missions conquered, lost, now lie
in a chest of envelopes, faint scent of petals,
locked. Illicit romance—nay? Play?
I am stitching on my tail when this hat is passed on
to me, a thief who can keep reveals.
It's the playwright of our holiday script
who moonlighted as a thespian, unraveling—
her latest side, another scrape.
She fidgets for a nugget from me.
Maybe when a pot of basil survives
a phase. Where to catch how that premium
on *happy* works. For now, I can mend pleats to puff
and she brews in our cube
for her chimera. Her seamstress who scoffs
at making music with a wild card. I confess—
asked to hone in on heart chakra,
my mind strays to kintsugi.
Her lore drifts into sewn mid-seasons. Mist fans
my monologue more fable than
the jest I fit. Every night I pause
after I fake a fall.
"Still here!"

WHY THE WARMTH

Summer, keeping me sheer eight months.
Fraying more knots until air. Next door slams
for the lastborn and breeze. She has her eye out for
a second ride, unaware she is a herald. So much light
from a dying sun, calluses scorch in loaned sandals. I am

all for lofty true, and wade in the low life.
An empath who won't charge to keep senses
heady is busking for change. The original rockers retire
in a shed for sanding. Boards, sometimes the odd armoire.
The right side of the brain can believe each piece, a note,

a curveball completes a puzzle when still a block.
Every other day, the highest of the year. A bruise blooms
above my knee. I reshape a leaf like I'm four or a fever
shading beyond lines. I blunt a pencil like I pick human
in a game. One lap in a pool before bleeding to next

month. The real child colors fruit of an absent season.
Like multiple choice by a cheat mate hiding
behind blue. When asked, he is cooler than moonlight.
The drops are seeds, he shrugs, go with a clue:
get the flow. My left hand grows a spot.

OCCLUSION

Some days, the whole day in the shower
like touch-me-nots folding the rest of a cold spell.
From rain or whose misplaced prod.

Some nights end like most
lives start, sensitive to light,
crying for no conclusive reason.

Ask lovers how light I am. A coverlet
between seasons. Ask loaners how dark I am. A pill
from a bassist precise, prescient, in algebra, in acrylic.

Where is the high sun burning through cracks
until shatter. When does a curse wafting through
alleys slide into a lexicon.

Deadlines, retrogrades clash. I'm included
in whose whisper voices
I could err better.

OF HANDS, ONE OUT THE WINDOW

I had not decided to stop speaking to you but the day rolled
on to the weekend I had to pick up my rescue, farther on to a series
of afterparties, a deal to close. Every ride led to a long walk.
I was emptying my screen of events. Night came to file signals
away. I wanted to rest my eyes on my steep autumn scene taken
from the raw side of a valley.
These were mountains that could not save villagers
from a plague. There is little satisfaction in deleting. Maybe none
in burning, but there is a moment to be thankful for—
when the flame warms your palms.
Before disappearing, I longed to feel your face. I fixed geranium
like iris on linoleum. It vanishes
easily in the mouth. Bon courage. Bonne chance.
Whichever is cool for a voyage. Cruel
you maybe felt, when I thought of you crying out
in a car, how much you needed me in those outbursts, idled.
I had meant to put you off. "Take care" comes
naturally when you've done the work like you have
sold all your belongings. But the next morning was full of codes.
You are a maze, you once said
in the same breath you were almost yelling you were not some sort
of bad person, knowing I was waiting for you to say
you just wanted your turn.
I was headed this direction, about processing, time unable to heal.
It was going to come out wrong so
I could apologize for one thing.
I did not plan to keep so quiet I don't know if you wondered
whether I had died. I have taken my rescue back out of town.
Maybe he has outgrown chewing, barking. I would not know
how to pacify an infant. I had mostly appetizers wherever I flew.
In Phnom Penh, I tried tarantulas.
So much has passed I am allowing carelessness, I feel full
of water, like I'm about to go deaf in an elevator.
Can't tell which stains are my oils.
No matter who is at the door I am willing to confess
I wrote those flyers, each one
lighter in tone than the others as letters fade.
I had not decided then to stop speaking, I do not think I did, to you
but I have already covered this. I still sink

what needs to be thawed. In a tangle being read
you still have my dial, yes, I have been informed and I want
my turn now,
I would like to place an order from the other side of the coast.

PACING IN

You fly with no cover but a date,
a city, of birth and origin
gazing outside like a child on a truck
burning a hole through hide, through tarp.

You wander where you can sleep sundering
sleeps in, the weekend to a year.
Alone at last, tossed alibi.
Your undershirt reeks of the last cure

you were paid to see through.
A needle and you can get by.
You can sing aloud a lullaby in a language
you did not know you knew by heart

as you do a strain you named your last name.
Nobody understands you and your map
shaped like an infected tree.
Everybody has a song to track down

deeper into the city.
Would you rather be unplugged sooner
than proven immortal?
You, drunk-dialing

with a phone book filled with ghosts.
You wind your times before diving
in a lake for culturing. Swallow
your sweat, tears.

Maybe you are an animal
comfortable in a storm until caged.
No voices to call out to you
in their jargon and gibberish.

Previewed sutures, would you rather
survive? You in nobody's bath,
shedding DNA, tiptoeing
on your chipped threshold.

LAND OF MAKESHIFT

And heatwave a sunstroke away. Two brothers
flood their den till they can drown
like urchins in a flash flood. Performance
an artist won't dissect. She peers
for a hose lost in the pool, limp lifeline once
haywire. More neighbors take
video as they would of dolphins.
Maybe siesta delays
a bulletin already in the air—
another summer followed by tremors, storm.
New fault. All summer a bug. Another two-lane over
roads like a new ordinance.
A road stretching bug season. Match to fever
of everyone in someone's sala
tuned in. The town drunks
don't make the cut to primetime
but the body count is not bad, on the bright side
no one missing today
from the next three streets. Nothing to see here,
strums ad lib like a compulsive piper and what is
riffing flows here, marring a ripple there, freestyling
freedom. Maybe just a hiker, his fading dog
in a shop cart. That last uphill.
Maybe *you're still here, right?*
—a chief to the needy. That last folly.
What is alright is relative. Elsewhere
a holy shroud hushes. Like our Sacred Heart
petal, claims an elder to empty seats.
Miracle: solar still on, outlasting attentions.
A cantina dins its stereo. Voiceover
assures their bread takes a minute but
a mother knows smoother cons.
When she was a mermaid in a fish tank

she smelled her mussels in her shower. Her youngest
asks why they can't do ice cream once.
Her middle of seven pinches her pill
for the blur or a wider evening
not to kick in. "Because no one kneads a scoop—"
she shrugs, trying to make herself laugh
away a sand boil inside her.

BORDER

Everybody has a threshold. Edge of urges,
        cut clean to go full circle. Crop out
               your dizzying clauses until you are hungry again.

Deep down you are far from lost. Just behind a finish
line fluttering like a kite caught.
        You don't listen to a recording left you when you are sure
        to play it over and over. You have had a taste of broken.

        But you won't see how far you will go if you do not
find what you have held on to.
        A spider makes itself scarce as you switch off.
Architect. Assassin.
        May your life be blessed with ease.

A parting shot is intended when it's flight. No shame
in owning the bit of rabid fury that has not grown bitter.

        Do you still leave yourself codes to mine?
        You had just turned teen when your list felt like
system: new dice, tourniquet 11:30
        wind breaker
          Ararat
      hearsay & alibi (look up, make up).
Maybe you have had your kingdom. A cycle is not the first

you see. Maybe you would understand best
        a newborn finding a thumb. You start with the cry
        of a flock crossing over. Try to open your mouth
          when your mother is lighter from you, severed.

CONFLATION IN LONGHAND WEATHER

I would take pride in those days that observed symmetry, also
the element of surprise. Every summer, there is a child who learns a
new word daily for the feeling of being dealt a card.

: *pizzicato*

I listen to a neighbor now for the time. Her bowl of macadamias
like worry beads. When movies ran from brunch to the last train,
she would head out at 4. She still catches daylight, waters
hibiscus she cannot keep from withering. Her prayer
was the rose-pink variety until her hair started graying years
from retirement. She meets the trails earlier than a family
with a bread maker. Till cocktail hour, she lunches with a couple
who would invite for golf, then snooker. Some weigh to see.
They joke *you can't be an alcoholic if you drink past 6*. Sometimes
she fine-tunes *it's 5 o'clock somewhere*. By primetime,
plate empty. Three children led by her dog, circling the block.

When I could have said this got me "ontological"
the solstice was followed by sand boils. People rushed out back
then at aftershocks. Desks were made heavier then, too.
The pine scent in a cabin takes me back to school. Lightnings
we counted late Fridays. Early Mondays, twisted crunches.
I practiced on my clarinet that made me draw
a chariot. Some vespers I heard from a grill station. I felt
a graveyard shift would be cool.

: *ricochet*

Some shadows are still out, listening for the main line.
I mix up times. But I can tell the mothers of those who drive around
to race as it gets cooler, from the handful who have had it but are
far from over, who hope to stop a dispatcher for directions.

PENDING

You have no child in your clip
for your wall. Childhood fills in for reflection
in the yard. Every sundown a December dimming
a lamp, your mother's cautionary tales
mixing parable and medical the way
she stuffed all she gleaned in a pie you can't
make from scratch beyond your smokes, a fog
you can't place when you first struck.
You are all set to do you again, fess up on video for
a fuck so deep you watch your claw
from above. Not hard to stand in for ghosts.
You have outdone you. The hunger that is your pride
has no digging to go but drill into older wounds.
You dream of the rings inside a redwood.
Your thumb you traded for
shingles, crates to shuck, a view to the pond
part of an ocean that in a storm threatens
to swallow. So time does.
You won't sit in a pantry across a handler
searching your gaze if you have rebuilt
your life in seven days.
When you are found clinging to a rail like a rope
for a swing, who can decide
which half to tear first, which eye can still be good.
Limbo tolls where you end, when
only your grandmother whistled your name
as you crawled to a spot sunlight found for warmth.

VIOLET HOUR

Thyme shoots, dragon fruit sorbet,
the market not marked by season or place.
A spigot for pots of chai. Free sun golds.
No one will think to look here, a hobby
city with no knobs. You can stop asking which
lengths can be seen. You are always seeing faces on
tenements with no numbers, in the simple-
knuckled branches where parking ends, where you
once pictured desires ripen. It's *makrut* here,
you need to repeat. Your head down, your gut
warmed. Only the three graces are more still.
To mock or beckon, their marble scalds then
cools like neither. Tomorrow, you are to stir
in kaffir lime. You dunk your face in their fountain.
A mirage of a memory retains. When you docked,
myths quivered beneath their bones.
You have cradled the receiver long, through
the night. Each seaside is overcast. How you
scan obituaries like wanted ads yet
no one is paying for a face with your name.
What to be but etched on the square. Free
and not all freedoms are for harming,
to heal. You feel ripe peppers, potatoes shaped
half a house or an ear. Inner stalls not caves.
Your chat with an herbalist on motion
sickness, a tattoo balm, takes you on deck,
the peak of a champagne pyramid.
A jilted love song sways your limbs
away from your heart. On the brink of rain,
flavors burn the air blue.

DISREMEMBERING

if this field could be a whole plot again, unravished, famished

if I could go back to every room, speak as willfully but be right

if I had that shoulder once more instead of these shadows

if to conceive were still a risk

if I could burn the ash growing marigolds

if no one wept at *never again*

if I could remember leaving my cave unlocked

if I had not had my spirit broken, if I could sign my body over to
    science

if this limb would not grow crooked from its trim

if I could mother into sobriety

if nights would not leave a clammy aubade

if we had endeavored trade if not truce

if sonnets would not drop from my palm

if I could wash out a bruise with a coat of flesh

ACKNOWLEDGMENTS

The author gratefully acknowledges the publications where these poems first appeared, some in other form:

arc{hive} – "Before Some Mud," "Of Hands, One Out the Window," "Say Nothing September,"
"Which Era Did You Want to Live In?"
Atlanta Review – "Day of the Eased Out," "Misappreciation Under Lockdown"
California Quarterly – "Why the Warmth"
Crosswinds Poetry Journal – "I Keep Myself Alone for You"
filling Station – "In the Dark, There Is No Half"
Great River Review – "Asked to Draw My Face," "Occlusion"
Gulf Stream Magazine – "Violet Hour"
Plainsongs Poetry Magazine – "White Screen"
Red Rock Review – "Moving On"
River Heron Review – "Hiatus"
Running with Water Anthology – "Pressed Flowers"
SMEOP – "Lighter Reds, Fading Blue," "Missing Some Blue in the Green"

Gratitude to Amy England, Amelia Martens.

Appreciation and gratitude to the following works and their creators that inspired some poems:

Films of Martin Rejtman; *Tatort: Streets of Berlin*; *Les Temps qui changent*; *Tabi no Owari Sekai no Hajimari*, and other superb works the author cannot recall.

Love and gratitude to my husband.

Thank you to my father and mother.

Thank you to my constant reader Meg, and to my wonderful nieces, Elise and Solene.

Thank you to my family and friends.

Kris Falcon's poems appear in *The Hong Kong Review*, *Atlanta Review*, *Gulf Stream Magazine*, and elsewhere. She is the author of *Alunsina's Wrist*. She received her MFA at the School of the Art Institute of Chicago.

I am struck by the variation in these pieces, the different line lengths and stanza/enjambment structures happening…. there is an admirable confidence and certainty in the various speaking voices I hear operating…a willingness, too, to risk something with memory…and retelling of memories…"

-Dave Sims, Editor, *The Raw Art Review*

The poems in Kris Falcon's *some blue, a little spur* function like a map of dark watercolors, where the speaker is building a way through a space-time collage. "You say there is nothing there. I see a lake...// I see how I am to depart." The pathfinding work of Falcon is grounded in logic, and the surreal nature of reality holds the reader in shared experience, for instance of being in lockdown, "We are stepping out after 36 weeks of showering / at sundown." Falcon carries us across a landscape where, "Any piece of fabric can look like / a body after a storm" and asks that we accept the lack of certainty, the fact that "Nobody understands you and your map / shaped like an infected tree." This collection holds both our felt experience of not having the answers, and requires our acknowledgement of how that "muscles what heals."

-Amelia Martens, author of *The Spoons in the Grass are There to Dig a Moat*

In floating night rooms, in untethered cities, Kris Falcon's poems construct, line by line, an architecture of subjective states of singularly detailed, melancholy beauty.

-Amy England, author of *Rooms Colors Dreams*

For additional titles by UnCollected Press please visit the following webpage:

https://therawartreview.com/books-for-sale/

www.ingramcontent.com/pod-product-compliance
Lightning Source LLC
Chambersburg PA
CBHW022037090426
42741CB00007B/1108